How to Spell Presbyterian

Newly Revised Edition

D0029719

James W. Angell

With a Foreword by Clifton Kirkpatrick

G
GENEVA

Geneva Press
Louisville, Kentucky

Scripture quotations, unless otherwise indicated, are from the New Revised Standard Version of the Bible, copyright © 1989 by the Division of Christian Education of the National Council of the Churches of Christ in the U.S.A. and are used by permission.

Book design by Sharon Adams
Cover design by The Printed Image Design Studio

Published by Geneva Press
Louisville, Kentucky

This book is printed on acid-free paper that meets the American National Standards Institute Z39.48 standard. ♾

PRINTED IN THE UNITED STATES OF AMERICA

06 07 08 09 10 11 — 10 9 8 7 6 5 4 3

Library of Congress Cataloging-in-Publication Data

Angell, James W.
  How to spell Presbyterian / James W. Angell; with a foreword by Clifton Kirkpatrick.—Newly rev. ed.
    p. cm.
  ISBN-13: 978-0-664-50196-9 (alk. paper)
  ISBN-10: 0-664-50196-6 (alk. paper)
    1. Presbyterian Church—Doctrines. 2. Presbyterian Church (U.S.A.)—Doctrines. I. Title.

BX8969.5.A54 2002
285'.137—dc21   2002023640

Publisher's Note

*T*he first edition of Jim Angell's classic *How to Spell Presbyterian* was published in 1977; the last revision was completed in 1984, just after Reunion.

In the ensuing years, there have been some changes in the Presbyterian Church (U.S.A.) that necessitated the updating of some of the factual information in this book. Also, not surprisingly, a few new acronyms have been added to the church's vocabulary. These are reflected in the updated glossary at the back of the book. This edition also contains a wonderful new foreword from the Stated Clerk of the PC(USA), the Rev. Clifton Kirkpatrick.

That said, the heart of this book remains as Jim Angell wrote it twenty-five years ago: a testament to his knowledge of, and deep love for, the Presbyterian Church.

Contents

Foreword

*F*irst published in 1977, this little book by Jim Angell has sold thousands of copies through the years. Those who have bought and read the book have been amply rewarded, because it is written in a breezy, easy-to-read style, yet packed with a whole host of informative facts, insights, and perspectives.

The fascinating thing is that a reader hardly notices that so much is informative and factual, as the material oozes out the way toothpaste emerges from a full tube onto the brush. All of a sudden a person is ready to brush the teeth (recognize that a great deal has been learned) with that clean and smiley sensation, fully aware that the tube is ready with so much more for next time.

With simple poems and deft illustrations, Angell gives us insights and understanding about the Presbyterian Church, how it functions and why, how positions have been developed, and how convictions have emerged.

The story is told, for instance, of how 1,700 years ago a man named Cyprian wrote about commitment: "It is knowing from the top of our heads down to our shoe buckles that private Christianity is an incongruity; it is believing that we are constantly meeting Christ in one another, and being blessed and identified as children of worth through such meetings." No sermon here, but the clear explanation that the

Christian faith as expressed in the Presbyterian Church is a community, not just an individual, experience, and that each one of us has a definite responsibility to be supportive of and to care for each of God's other creatures.

Something of the same theme and message are stressed when the subject of election and ordination of ministers and church officers is under discussion. "Election and ordination represent not so much the granting of honor as the assumption of responsibility. It has been said that ordination does not mean so much the laying on of hands as it does the raising of hands." Anyone who has worked in a church as an employee or as a volunteer is fully aware of the heartaches and rewards of such service. Further, "church work" is not just what happens inside the church walls, but how you regularly handle assignments, joys, and disappointments in the workaday world.

And so it goes, with the author teaching about the whole range of issues in the Presbyterian Church by using illustrative words and ideas, instead of boring definitions of what the specific words and ideas mean. Your eyes and mind just glide, absorbing without being fully aware that concepts and principles are being elucidated and interpreted.

This book, then, is for a wide range of readers, definitely including persons new to the Presbyterian Church and those who are newly elected, or even contemplating serving, as church officers or church leaders in any capacity. For those who already "know it all," the book is an excellent refresher course in Presbyterian 101, 201, and even 301, because the expression of realities is so fresh and dynamic that there is no sense of "I've been through all this routine stuff before." Each thing grabs the reader anew and with sparkling vitality.

To put it another way, the book is written in a lyrical fashion so that it sings; to put it still another way, the book is poetic. All through the book, the author literally breaks into poems to express his great spirit and joyful mood, to share with others the uplifting nature of the church of Jesus Christ.

The doctrines, the theology, the biblical bases, and the basic governmental underpinnings of the Presbyterian Church are not boring or treated with a heavy hand. These sometimes weighty subjects are not glossed over at all, but they are reviewed with such a depth of comprehension that the point of each subject or issue is clearly expressed in language that is not "preacher talk" nor street talk. Rather, Angell uses the conversational manner of a family sitting around the table talking informally after supper, or of a discussion group of alert and caring people in a thoughtful, meaningful Sunday school class.

So, in addition to being a significant brief book that covers a wide range of material for individual reflection, it is also the kind of book that lends itself to group consideration in a church officers' training event, a new members' class, or a typical class of young people that is interested in a serious treatment—in less than a dead-serious vein—of the faith as it is expressed and lived in the Reformed tradition called Presbyterian.

The original text has been revised and made current, because there have been many changes in the church since the book was first published. It is enriching, however, to recognize that the basic emphases and their treatment are just as valid now as the day they were written. Though details may change, the hard core—if one may use that term—of this book is timeless. That is the beauty of being a part of a continuing journey in community with others in the Reformed tradition of nearly five hundred years.

Clifton Kirkpatrick
Stated Clerk
Presbyterian Church (U.S.A.)

Introduction

Somebody is always asking how to spell *Presbyterian*.

Whether it's in connection with opening a new charge account or listing a religious preference, the questioner usually gets as far as the first three or four letters, then looks up sheepishly and inquires, "How do you *spell* Presbyterian?"

Presbyterian is more than a twelve-letter word.

It's also an important piece of the Christian story. It is a form of church government. It is an attitude about freedom and the people's responsibility for working out the content and expression of their faith. It is a commitment to care about people in trouble.

The title of this book refers to something more than learning the correct spelling of a word. It has to do with getting the hang of how we Presbyterians think and how we are joining our imagination, energies, resources, and spiritual independences to serve Jesus Christ.

It deals with what membership in the Presbyterian Church (U.S.A.) both offers and asks.

My own career as a Presbyterian began when I was eight or nine years old. The Presbyterian church was within walking distance of where my family lived. On Sunday mornings at ten minutes to nine I would hear its bells announcing that Sunday school was about to begin. I went. Nothing in my life since has made as much difference as that. The church was a small frame structure, served by a seminary student. There were no separate church school classrooms. It was rumored that one woman in the congregation was so wealthy, she put five dollars in the offering plate every Sunday!

This is a different time. A much different time. Yet it is the same world, and hope is as necessary as it ever was. Carl Sandburg once wrote that we are "born with rainbows" in our hearts, and I think he's right about that. But rainbows fade and are lost. They are forgotten and forfeited. Our technological triumphs are impressive beyond description: a space shuttle, genetic breakthroughs, electron microscopes, Viking telemetry from Mars, a whole brightly carpeted civilization. But the heart stays hungry. We still crave direction, meaning, freedom, dignity, and love—things money cannot buy, but which constitute the spiritual stonework on which the church is built.

Regardless of which door you came through, this book assumes you have found your way inside and that you want to learn more about Presbyterian traditions of faith and government. I hope it helps achieve that goal.

James W. Angell, Pastor
Claremont Presbyterian Church
Claremont, California

Chapter 1

Some Key Ideas

*H*ere are a few key ideas with which to get started.

We Worship God

Presbyterians are guided in their worship both by apostolic practice and by Protestant Reformers of the sixteenth and subsequent centuries.

The spiritual revolutionaries of the sixteenth century—we usually name Martin Luther and John Calvin, although there were others—stressed the priesthood of all believers in contrast to the separate, professional priesthood that had dominated the church for more than one thousand years. The Reformation found its models for change and renewal in the New Testament and said *all* believers were to be ministers and interpreters of Jesus Christ.

Our worship draws upon the full biblical tradition of God's people assembling for praise, prayer, and instruction—and then going out to share the joys and responsibilities of an informed discipleship. There is a rhythm here of gathering and dispersing, which discredits the notion that the true business of the church is one or the other.

We combine ancient liturgies with newer, more casual and

imaginative forms, but the goal remains the same: to proclaim the good news of salvation and to invite all who hear to follow and serve Jesus Christ. One section of our Constitution is called Directory for Worship. There, worship is defined as both proclamation and response. Useful guidelines are provided for the ordering of corporate worship, the administering of the sacraments, the planning of the music of worship, and the place of weddings and funerals (better called services of witness to the resurrection) in the total witness of the Christ community.

Worship may be awesome, fun, comforting, or disturbing. At different times in our lives, it probably ought to be all four of these experiences.

It has been called God's party, a festival of meaning that includes One who is the life of the party. "Joy," someone has said, "is the flag that flies from the citadel of the soul to show that the Spirit of God is in residence."

After a hymn of adoration, we often confess our sin in unison as the natural consequence of finding ourselves in the presence of a God who judges us with love.

Sometimes we use the word *confession* to mean something else, to refer positively to statements of conviction. Many churches are nonconfessional. They affirm the Scriptures but no other creeds or summaries of truth. Our church is confessional. Our *Book of Confessions* contains a number of the best-known, most-used confessions, beginning with the Apostles' Creed (second century) and including a relatively recent testimony of faith and concern that carries its date (deliberately so) in the title: the Confession of 1967. Such statements help anchor us in a history that has helped to make us Christian. They are useful road maps for guiding the church without falsely restricting it or violating one of its most cherished ideas: that Jesus Christ is Sovereign over each conscience.

We observe two sacraments: baptism, which celebrates our entrance into the family, and the Lord's Supper, which celebrates Christ's perpetual resurrection presence among us.

Presbyterians are also people who pray—singly and together. Prayer is God's spirit touching and shaping human spirit. Sometimes it is gratitude. At other times, it is a cry for help. It is love and hope, a bridge to heaven, a golden sash around the earth. It rebukes our quarreling and wars, our sins and loneliness. It summons us to wholeness.

Prayer is more than some form of mortal instinct. It is the exercise of choice—the choice to open the doors of our hearts to listen, to unclench our hands to serve.

The president of one of our theological seminaries once listed six distinctive characteristics of Presbyterian churches. He developed his list not out of books but out of the experience of visiting many congregations over a period of time. He concluded that there is an element of predictability as to what one can expect to find in a typical Presbyterian church.

He spoke first of a sense of majesty in worship, second of traditionally strong preaching, and third of the shared leadership of the service, involving laity as well as gowned ministers. Fourth, he named the presence of a church school, adult forums, and study groups. Fifth, church bulletins that call attention to community needs and social matters. And sixth, that ubiquitous prayer of confession—so very Presbyterian.

In my experience I think I have more questions raised about the prayer of confession than any other detail of the liturgy. But in the Presbyterian tradition we have never been able to exalt God without at the same time being made conscious of—not in a condemning, but in a cleansing, liberating way—our own sin.

Jesus Is Sovereign

Not all Presbyterians interpret doctrine in the same way. We are united not by monolithic theology but by our mutual need for the forgiveness of sins, a representative system of government, and a shared ministry of helping and healing.

And we are one in proclaiming Jesus Christ to be Sovereign and Savior of our lives. We declare that we have found new life in Christ—new life as individuals, new life together.

Although all Presbyterians do not answer the great questions that have to do with God, humankind, and the world in exactly the same way, we have for more than four hundred years been making the following case for the claims of Jesus Christ:

- *The God of the Christian revelation is Sovereign of history.* God acts through history, cares about it, and wants us to care about it. God is not chiefly understood as an essence to be contemplated, but as a sovereign to be enjoyed and served.
- *God sent Jesus into the world, not to condemn it but to save it.* Jesus is the promised Christ—not the Messiah who was expected, but the one who uniquely reveals God as the love that will not let us go, that will not let us down, and that will not let us off.
- *We are saved by grace* rather than by good deeds, correct beliefs, or human ceremonies. Salvation is unearnable. It can only be accepted with thanksgiving and joy. Grateful persons are too busy being grateful to hate.
- *Jesus is Liberator.* He frees us from the tyranny of ourselves, the tyranny of tyrants, the tyranny of systems—including theological ones.
- *We need one another.* We cannot be human alone, or Christian alone. A private Christianity is an impossibility.
- *We are both the reconciled and the reconciling.* Jesus has commissioned us to continue his work. We pray: "Make me bread, Lord; break me up and pass me around."

Love without Justice Isn't Love

The Presbyterian Church (U.S.A.) (that's our official name) is committed to seeking complete justice for all persons.

Love and justice form a single truth. The church's agenda is life rather than religion.

We are unwilling to be relegated to the periphery of the human discussion concerning destiny.

We do not wish to evade the world's ugliness and pain. We believe God is calling us to reshape human life, to save Earth from suicide, and to undertake the adventures of the future reverently and expectantly.

We are uneasy about using the word *spiritual*. In its best connotation, however, we not only use it but exult in it.

God is Spirit. And the spirit of humankind is the candle of God.

But our orientation is more Hebrew than Greek. We are earthy in our interests and caring. We are concerned with hunger, disease, greed, violence, and plundering. We seek true fulfillments for our sexuality and technological genius.

Reinhold Niebuhr, one of the most admired and listened-to theologians of the first half of the twentieth century, wrote: "Love without power simply surrenders the world to power without love. How to make power express love, and love humanize power, is the distinctive task of the Church of Christ for the next hundred years."

Presbyterians do not usually understand prophecy as clairvoyance. Rather, we think of it as a way of looking at life through the eyes of the prophets and of Jesus; describing what we feel and see; feeling the hurt, frustration, and despair of millions; and seeing the new world that is possible because Jesus has come with his call for brave, world-transforming responses to suffering and evil.

All Things Are to Be Done Decently and in Order

Our authority is expressed corporately rather than personally.

We place authority in ordered groups elected by the people,

believing God works through groups in significant ways. We choose moderators rather than presidents.

We do a great deal of voting.

We are wise enough to know the majority isn't always right. Still, in keeping with our trust in the ability of the Holy Spirit to speak and work through the many, we put great confidence in the corporate decisions of those who have studied the Word, prayed their prayers, learned from life and one other. Motivated supremely by a love for God, and responsive to their own minds and hearts above everything else, they vote their understanding of heaven's will.

The word *Presbyterian* is from the Greek word *presbyteros,* which means "elder."

Some branches of Christianity are named for beliefs or practices that have been singled out for special emphasis: Baptists for "believer's baptism"; Catholics for their teaching concerning the universal, continuous character of the organized church. Lutherans bear the name of Martin Luther. Congregationalists, Episcopalians, and Presbyterians are named for styles of government. Congregationalism approaches pure democracy, most decisions being made by the congregation as a whole. Episcopacy is an arrangement that includes large powers for bishops. Presbyterianism locates most responsibility in groups of representative Christians, including both elders (laity) and ministers of the Word (clergy).

The office of elder has a long history. It figures prominently in the story of the wilderness travels of the Israelites and often in the correspondence of Paul, eighteen hundred years later. *Presbyteros* occurs seventy-two times in the New Testament and refers to persons charged with teaching the faith, ironing out troubles, and helping God's exodus community continue safely on its way.

At the *local* level, elders are elected by the congregation to serve collectively as the *session.* At the *area* level, they serve as commissioners to *presbyteries.* On a *regional* level, they serve as commissioners to *synods,* and *nationally,* as commissioners to the *General Assembly.*

Within these governing bodies debate is frequently intense. But this is not something for which we feel apology is due. Rugged but respectful exchanges of opinion often constitute the best way to find acceptable answers to complex problems. God as Holy Spirit is our final arbiter, and we seek such leading in humility, love, and hope.

Presbyterian government is connectional and interdependent. Its bone structure is its Constitution, which has two parts: Part I is the *Book of Confessions,* a collection of eleven historically significant faith statements spanning about eighteen hundred years. Part II is the *Book of Order*—a manual for regulating church life and resolving conflict.

Sessions, presbyteries, and synods are not thought of as separate cooperating units, but as "slices of one loaf."

Therefore, a question new members may be called upon to answer asks: "Will you seek the fellowship of the church wherever you may be?" Christ is one. So is Christ's church.

Freedom and authority are thus combined in a remarkable way. We might doubt that a church that insists on the right of each member to work out answers, with Jesus Christ as the sole judge of the rightness of those answers, could ever wind up working intimately in any tightly knit unity. We are, perhaps, like the bumblebee whose tiny wingspan and heavy body structure make it aerodynamically impossible to fly. The bumblebee ignores this and flies anyway.

The Church Exists
by Mission as Fire Exists by Burning

Not missions but *mission.*

Mission is the work of Jesus wherever it is done and by whomever it is done.

We do not understand the church to be the only tool God can use. The church has another role, too, as the announcer of God's activity, which may be going on in surprising places, carried on by surprising people.

God may be involved in your life now in ways you don't suspect.

As catalyst.

As advocate for those too weary or powerless to wage the fight for justice on their own.

As physician, friend, teacher, farmer, lawyer, cook, or artist wielding the brush of vision.

Before machinery and speeds of Mach 2 shrank the earth, there were still "foreign countries." Before interstellar satellites, the end of colonialism, and our consciousness of American pluralism, Sandwich Islands types of "missions" (it usually meant some place to speak the Word considerably removed from where we stood) made sense. We sent people on long journeys to win souls, mend bodies, teach minds. And they performed superbly.

We had missionary societies, missionary budgets.

Now a new situation prevails.

Today most overseas churches are indigenous—controlled by the native born. A developing nation sends personnel and spiritual insight to a more affluent West. There also exists the awareness that the opportunity and chance to "do" mission is at everyone's fingertips.

Congregations don't wait for "mission" appeals from official headquarters; they unearth all sorts of such opportunities in their own backyards.

Yet we Presbyterians support mission on six continents—often as ecumenical partners, occasionally by ourselves (see chapter 3). We won't wait until things are all set right at home to respond to a huge imbalance of life's abundances.

We seek to avoid the weakness inherent in piecemeal approaches to mission by combining forces through the agencies of the General Assembly Council.

Dare to Hope

Our family once received the popular game Trivial Pursuit for Christmas. We had a lot of fun playing it. Players move around a gameboard obstacle course by asking and answering questions in six categories. Questions like "How many players are on a lacrosse team?" Or "Who invented radar?" Or "Which American president was the first to ride in an airplane?"

Sometimes the church seems to play the trivia game, as it fusses over rules and argues over doctrine, and winds up immersed in institutional housekeeping.

But the real agenda of faith is not trivial. When it asks, "What must I do to be saved from a life of emptiness, greed, fear, and doubt?" or, "If a man dies, will he live again?" or, "Is there any word from the Lord?" or, Jesus' question, "Who do you say that I am?" triviality is put aside. We begin to deal with the great human questions of identity, meaning, and hope.

We Presbyterians don't have all the answers. But we can say what we believe:

We believe God holds the future.

We believe we must pray and work together—be something as well as organizing to *do* something.

We do not underrate the power of the satanic or the danger that characterizes our nuclear tomorrows.

But no one has any more authentic word of encouragement and direction to speak to an anxious, half-hungry/half-overweight, wondering world than do we. We are rainbow people, torchbearers who sing as we march, who laugh as we die.

Predestination, often associated with Presbyterian thinking, rather than suggesting a fatalistic "whatever will be will be," is a powerful summons to strive. It does not play down our responsibility for the future, nor does it imagine it fixed. What it does is set those efforts in a larger context. It says that destiny will be finally settled more by God's love than by our wit. In the long run, God's purposes prevail. Our efforts will be used—as were Moses' and Miriam's; so will our dreams—as were Mary's and Joseph's. But God's program will never be held hostage to our uncertain resolution, forgetfulness, selfishness, failure, or limited talent.

The future is God's.

And we are Christ's.

Such confidence frees us to get on with both our service and our singing, our exploitation of all the territories of hope, our whole confettied parade down the thoroughfares of time.

Chapter 2

Commitment

A Leap and a Rescue

*I*t was a Sunday afternoon in early November.

Lorraine Harrison had gone to the garage to locate a cleaning rag when she noticed the new bicycle she and her husband had bought for their son's birthday. On an impulse she decided to try it out for herself—take a quick spin around the block.

As she wheeled down the street, suddenly she became aware of a commotion at one of the houses she was passing. A woman ran out of the house, crying: "Baby drowning. No swim!"

Laying the bike down quickly, Lorraine followed the woman to the back of the house where she saw two men struggling in the middle of a swimming pool. Neither could swim. She would also discover later that neither could speak English.

She stopped only to remove her wristwatch and jumped in. She clung to the side of the pool and extended a hand to the men, successfully pulling them in.

Meanwhile the mother cried again, "No baby!"

Lorraine went to the deep end but couldn't see the child for the murkiness of the water. She dived in anyway.

The next thing she remembered was pushing on the baby's stomach.

Three-year-old Ronnie Fakhoury was bloated and blue. Lorraine tried the kiss of life—mouth-to-mouth resuscitation. She thought of calling the fire department, but there was no telephone in the house. There were, however, keys in a car parked close by. She showed the father and mother how to continue the mouth-to-mouth method, and the four of them took off in a panic for the hospital.

They were stopped by police for running a red light at seventy miles an hour, transferred to the police car, and taken to a hospital. The boy survived.

When Ronnie had fallen in, the father, heedless of his own safety, had leaped in to save him. An uncle, standing close by, also a nonswimmer, had sought to save the father. Lorraine Harrison had saved them all.

Commitment is both a leap and a rescue.

It is God's act of invading love represented by the coming of Jesus Christ into human life.

And our response of discipleship.

However awkwardly we may try to explain what commitment is, it is something at the opposite end from indifference.

It is the opposite of death.

The opposite of greed and anxiety.

The opposite of "letting George do it."

The opposite of boredom. The opposite of a safe, silky creature-comfort world built exclusively around our own pleasure.

On the positive side, it is the Spirit of God inviting us to change a message about resurrection from an Easter sermon into the 365-days-a-year stuff of life.

It is an electricity flowing through our souls and a power busy accomplishing something in the world.

It is a commitment to honesty of life.

It is life's most important yes—our saying yes to a God who has said yes to us in Jesus. Church membership is the setting in which we keep testing and improving the quality of that yes.

We no longer speak about conversion so readily as we

once did. Perhaps conversion became too suggestive of a flimflam sawdust trail, or of Damascus Road experiences that, although convincing and life-transforming for a few, did not, for many, explain the nature of their encounter with Christ. Their meeting was often a subtler thing—associated with questions of identity, with some winsome quality they saw in others who had come to know Jesus and had determined to pin their hopes on and pledge their lives to him, with something ethically compelling about the man from Galilee, or with a light they didn't even know existed until they were called upon to travel some personal road of tragic darkness.

Commitment has become our replacement word for conversion. And we may be the poorer for that if, in the exchange, we have lost the radical element of decision—moving out of an old state of crumbling death into a new state of total and abiding aliveness.

Life involves us in various philosophical discussions that seem to go on forever. Eventually, though, we come to the bottom line. There we must choose whether life for us is yes or no, whether we will elect to believe that a thread of purpose runs through this fabric we call history, or whether such a claim, down in the bedrock of our brain, is mere wishing—illusion, cowardly projection.

Commitment is lining up on the side of unproved truth. There is no way to prove beyond doubt that Jesus is the Messiah, God in Christ. Or that following him won't get us more trouble, rather than happy payoffs. He warned those who expressed interest in following him that the cost would be high (Matt. 10:34–39). It would be a mistake, especially in an era of considerable disinterest in organized religion, to attempt to lure the reluctant by letting on that entry into a life of discipleship isn't all that big a deal.

It is.

It has always been.

Commitment is voluntary. It is the free, undivided act of mind and heart.

Of the more than six billion people on earth, no one can make the decision you make, because no one can be who you are.

A man held a live bird in his hands cupped behind his back.

Thinking to deceive another, he asked, "Is it dead or alive?"

If his acquaintance guessed "alive," he planned to crush the bird with a silent, unobservable squeeze. He would then hold out the small dead form, proving the guesser wrong.

If "dead," his thought was to open his hands and let the bird fly free.

Either way he felt in control of the outcome.

But his friend, to his surprise, answered, "It is as you will."

Commitment is a choice. A stepping forward to be counted. Then a process of endless becoming.

Commitment is a life to live, not simply a statement to make. Yet it must have a moment of starting, of birth.

These questions, often asked of those making a public commitment, are beautifully plain:

Q: _____, who is your Lord and Savior?

A: Jesus Christ is my Lord and Savior.

Q: Do you trust in him?

A: I do.

Q: Do you intend to be his disciple, to obey his Word, and to show his love?

A: I do.

Q: Will you be a faithful member of this congregation, giving of yourself in every way, and will you seek the fellowship of the church wherever you may be?

A: I will.

Then follow some words of confirmation:

> _____, you are a disciple of Jesus Christ. He has commissioned you. Live in his love, and serve him.
>
> Be filled with gratitude. Let the message of Christ dwell among you in all its richness. Whatever you are doing, whether you speak or act, do everything in the name of the Lord Jesus, giving thanks to God the Father through him.

This is our moment of send-off and salvation, of putting on what J. B. Phillips calls "the clean fresh clothes of the new life" (Eph. 4:24).[1]

Baptism was the promise that this fullness of relationship would be part of our life as a Christian.

Now it has become our own.

It represents life's most important yes.

Silence is the equivalent of no.

I loved the way the breakfast-hour television show _Today_ used to open with outdoor cameras panning across the New York City skyline through the gray half-light of early morning.

Below, on Manhattan's streets, we could see yellow taxis scoot through concrete canyons. Along other noisy, narrow thoroughfares, vans pulled alongside curbs to unload.

Tugs on the East River, like little pipe-smoking gnomes, hauled barges loaded with oil drums past Pier 80.

Through a pale-blue scrim of haze, like someone yawning awake, the Big Apple welcomed the arrival of another day.

An on-street camera would show us an Ingmar Bergman procession of faces. Everyone in a hurry, intent on keeping rendezvous with another person or waiting task. Occasionally we saw the flicker of a smile, but it was usually pretty early for that. More often, emotions were in neutral and eyes straight ahead.

Then the crowds thickened. Bring up the gain on the background music. Wait for the stoplight. Forward again. Two more blocks. The elevator. The fifteenth floor. The familiar greeting. The familiar desk. The familiar lunch.

Out at Kennedy, early flights were lined up waiting for "clear for takeoff." Below ground, subway trains were emptying out more humanity en route to the banquet of life.

Not all of us live in metropolitan areas like New York. Some of us live in grassier places, in the presence of wheat fields, or with snow-topped mountains at our back. Some of us work in supermarkets in Springfield, or in insurance offices in Des Moines. Some of us teach in high school or college classrooms. We drive trucks. Manage homes. Operate X-ray equipment.

But all are part of God's procession.

We are all vessels outward bound, in transit between birth and death.

Passengers on a spaceship—walking the decks beneath a boundless sky. Asking, "What's it all about?" And "Why?"

Christianity thinks it knows, and it presents us with an offer.

Its claims are both modest and stunning.

Modest because the Christian faith does not pretend to supply answers to all questions and is not ashamed because it cannot.

Stunning because for those who embrace its affirmations and identify with its mission, the question "What is the purpose of living?" is answered not vaguely, but decisively and heart-spinningly in Jesus Christ.

Christ is God's good news *to us.*

Christ is God *with us.*

Out of such recognition a thousand wonders flow. And in such recognition our membership in the church begins.

The life-renewing, front-page-of-the-heart information that gets at the root problem of human life—the problem of self-worth—is that the God who created us continues to have a terribly deep interest in us.

Accepted and loved by God, we can live each day in confidence and for ends greater than some private and perishable version of success.

The gospel, sometimes summarized as "God so loved the world that he gave his only Son" (John 3:16) and at other times by "in Christ God was reconciling the world to himself" (2 Cor. 5:19), is a laser beam burning its way through an overcast of sin and a sometimes almost unbearable ambiguity of things we cannot understand.

A newspaper carries the report of a young man who, despondent over the breakup of a two-year-old marriage, bought a gun and killed seven people in a university library in less than ten minutes. Some were known to be among his closest friends.

Hunger stalks parts of the globe while an American connoisseur spends $14,000 for a rare bottle of wine.

In spite of such cruel data, and aware that other centuries have contained even more appalling accounts of seeming injustices and contradictions of a properly managed universe, those who call themselves Christ's people continue to believe and to trust a good God.

Presbyterians are part of this company. Their Reformed heritage is special, but their membership is in a universal society of hope.

Helmut Thielecke, German theologian and parish pastor, says that for those who have eyes of faith, history moves simultaneously on two levels.

One forms its bass clef. On this lower register, the ebb and flow of fortune and misfortune continue. Ships put to sea.

Governors govern. Graduates march to "Pomp and Circumstance," grow older, and have children who do the same thing. Seed is planted, harvested, planted again, "Sunrise, sunset, swiftly fly the years!" Hellos and good-byes. An eternal wash of years.

Joseph and Mary make the trip to Jerusalem for a tax enrollment. The innkeeper works out an overnight arrangement. The shepherds come. They look, marvel, and leave. A baby cries. A star looks down. A donkey brays, and the sound is lost on a Bethlehem wind.

But there's also a treble clef, says Dr. Thielecke. On this upper level, another faint melody can be heard. A divine purpose is unfolding. A counterpoint is at work, helping to form a harmony.

Christians are people who believe life is symphonic, and that their encounter with Jesus helps them know the score.

⚘⚘⚘⚘⚘⚘⚘

The finest compliment God has paid us is to create us free.

Freedom is volatile stuff, but there would be no way to tell the story of heaven's love or to narrate the history of the Presbyterian Church without exploration into that fragile wonder and into the striking accomplishment of representative self-government.

We are people of the Old Testament as well as the New, and, unless it is the absolute faithfulness of God, no theme dominates these complementary writings more than the struggle of people to become free, to stay free in the face of various tyrannies.

Exodus and exile are the two great hinges of history upon which the Old Testament swings. When we come to the New Testament, the struggle in a sense appears unchanged. Only now the oppressor is religion itself. The human spirit wears but another cast of chains.

That's the bad news.

The good news is that the demands that form the committed life turn out to be the realities that set us free, that free us from a frosty forfeiture—emptiness and greed—and from a hotter kind of hell—fear and guilt.

Life that has no demands at all made upon it is the life that is in the sorriest danger.

A sign in a corporate office warns others not to bring any good news there. It is partly put-on but contains glints of seriousness as it goes on to explain that good news may become an invitation to complacency. Bad news can call us to battle, ask us to fight back with courage, strength, and toughness.

Liberated from loneliness and lostness, Jesus gives us a banner to carry and sets us in the middle of a community of meaning.

The Confession of 1967 (Inclusive Language Text) avows:

> This life, death, resurrection, and promised coming of Jesus Christ has set the pattern for the church's mission. His human life involves the church in the common life of all. His service to men and women commits the church to work for every form of human well-being. His suffering makes the church sensitive to all the sufferings of humanity so that it sees the face of Christ in the faces of people in every kind of need. His crucifixion discloses to the church God's judgment on our inhumanity to each other and the awful consequences of our own complicity in injustice. In the power of the risen Christ and the hope of his coming the church sees the promise of God's renewal of human life in society and of God's victory over all wrong.
>
> The church follows this pattern in the form of its life and in the method of its action. So to live and serve is to confess Christ as Lord.[2]

Faith also frees us from a dependence on violence to solve the problem of getting along together, or from being egotistically defensive.

It opens up the life of grace—life that is intensively motivated and controlled by gratitude.

> Dear Child—
> Morning explodes with joy at the thought of you.
> All the rose-gold points of the sunrise
> Are caught in your smile
> And the waves of your laughter
> Break on the day's fresh sand.
>
> You are the still, slender thread of hope,
> Circling and tying
> The broken world.
> You are remembrance;
> 　Tears and lost faces.
> You are tomorrow—and yesterday,
> 　Matched in your eyes.
>
> 　　You are Immanuel.
> 　　You are Messiah.
> 　　Child of Life's ground.
> 　　Dear Child.[3]

Commitment means taking on an identity, and this becomes an identifying with others.

It means entering into the hurts and struggles of the poor and rejected, the disfranchised, distraught, and disheartened.

It means coming to understand these struggles as our own, whether these adjectives fit our own condition of the moment or not.

It makes it possible for the incarnation to continue through the reality of our caring.

In a letter written seventeen hundred years ago from North Africa by a man named Cyprian to his friend Donatus, there is this poignant paragraph:

It is really a bad world, Donatus, an incredibly bad world. Yet in the midst of it I have found a quiet and holy people. They have discovered joy which is a thousand times better than any pleasure. They are despised and persecuted, but . . . they have overcome the world. These people, Donatus, are the Christians, and I am one of them.[4]

Commitment is walking together along a road that doesn't end.

It is suffering together, celebrating, reinforcing one another's impossible dreams.

It is checking out our understanding of God's will together—deciding how we can be obedient and magnificently obsessed in these days of our own years.

It is loving and allowing ourselves to be loved.

It is being merciful, and granting mercy—even to ourselves.

It is promises to keep, and promises that keep us.

It is knowing from the top of our heads down to our shoe buckles that private Christianity is an incongruity; it is believing that we are constantly meeting Christ in one another, and being blessed and identified as children of worth through such meetings.

In such interfaces the sounds of the upper register, like the big organ played on the mezzanine at Wanamaker's store in Philadelphia at Christmastide as shoppers mill below, fill all God's dazzling world with the music of shalom.

Chapter 3

Witness

Speaking and Doing

*W*hen the sultan of Oman decided to show friendship toward the United States, he sent President Martin Van Buren two Arabian horses, a case of rose perfume, five demijohns of cologne, a package of cashmere shawls, a bale of Persian rugs, a box of pearls, and a sword.

God did it differently.

God came as a child, born of woman, as is every child, yet clothed with God's power and name as no other.

To Joseph, God's angel said, of the child to be born to Mary, "You are to name him Jesus, for he will save his people from their sins" (Matt. 1:21).

He grew up in Nazareth.

He was killed in Jerusalem.

His resurrection from death was disputed and doubted, but the claim "Christ is risen!" has lighted a fire that still burns against the darkness and the cold.

The church's evangelism consists of telling this story and acting out its implications. The meaning of evangelism is to bear good news. This makes us all evangelists. Our daily life in the world *is* our evangelism.

A witness is someone with information that, when taken with the testimony of others, helps truth to emerge.

A witness is both compelled to speak and under obligation to *do.*

Presbyterians have been engaged in both speaking and doing for well over two hundred years. We have more than seven hundred mission representatives, who, in the name of over 2.5 million of us, work around the world. We are organized into 11,178 congregations, 173 presbyteries, and 16 synods. As of the year 2001, we had 21,065 ordained ministers of the Word and Sacrament.

We are related to sixty-seven colleges and universities, six secondary schools, and twelve theological seminaries.

We witness more by what we *are* than by what we *say* we are.

We are called to honor this Lord of ours in family relationships—and in political decisions. Together we seek, on behalf of our Leader, wholeness of life for all people and all societies of people, not just those on good terms with our political order.

And we do not settle for a role of impartiality. The weak need help more than the strong. We are their advocates as Jesus Christ is ours at the throne of grace.

A congregation in Ohio put a sign over the main church doorway: SERVANTS ENTRANCE.

We take the church seriously as suffering servant, called to identify with the cry of all who are in pain and to form ourselves into communities of caring and change. We deny that the essence of Christian piety is an introspective experience of well-being and self-service.

The heart of incarnation theology is that God is no transcendent sky dweller but is re-creating the world by walking beside us in fields, neoned streets, unemployment lines, hospital corridors, and legislative halls.

Presbyterians tend to identify with and support such statements as the following:

The transforming reality of God's reign is found today:

—In the struggles of the poor to gain a share of the world's wealth, to become creative participants in the common economic life, and to move our world toward an economic democracy of equity and accountability.

—In the transforming drive for ethnic dignity against the persistent racism of human hearts and social institutions.

—In the endeavor by women to overcome sexist subordination in the church's ministry, in society at large, and in the images that bind our minds and bodies.

—In the attempts within families to overcome prideful domination and degrading passivity, and to establish genuine covenants of mutuality and joyous fidelity.

—In the efforts by many groups to develop for modern humanity a love for its cities as centers of civility, culture, and human interdependence.

—In the demands of the sick and the elderly for inexpensive, accessible health care administered with concern, advised consent, and sensitivity.

—In the voices of citizens and political leaders who demand honesty and openness, who challenge the misplaced trust of the nation in might, and who resist the temptations to make a nation and its institutions objects of religious loyalty.

—In the research of science when it warns of dangers to humanity and quests for those forms of technology which can sustain human well-being and preserve ecological resources.

—In the humanities and social sciences when the depths of human meanings are opened to inquiry and are allowed to open our horizons, especially whenever there is protest against the subordination of religion to scientistic rationality or against the removal of religion from realms of rational discourse.

—In the arts where beauty and meaning are explored, lifted up, and represented in ways that call us to deeper sensibilities.

—In the halls of justice where righteousness is touched with mercy, when the prisoner and the wrongdoer are treated with dignity and fairness.

—And especially in those branches and divisions of the church where the truth is spoken in love, where transforming social commitments are nurtured and persons are brought to informed conviction, where piety is renewed and recast in concert with the heritage, and where such struggles as these here identified are seen as the action of the living God who alone is worshiped.[5]

Persons take their places in the Presbyterian Church (U.S.A.) in any one of three ways: a public profession of faith preceded or accompanied by baptism; the renewal of earlier vows, sometimes referred to as "reaffirmation of faith"; or a certificate of transfer from another church whose order and confessions are consistent with our own.

The meaning of membership is defined in the *Book of Order* as follows:

A faithful member accepts Christ's call to be involved responsibly in the ministry of his church. Such involvement includes:

- proclaiming the good news,
- taking part in the common life and worship of a particular church,
- praying and studying Scripture and the faith of the Christian church,
- supporting the work of the church through the giving of money, time, and talents,
- participating in the governing responsibilities of the church,
- demonstrating a new quality of life within and through the church,

- responding to God's activity in the world through service to others,
- living responsibly in the personal, family, vocational, political, cultural, and social relationships of life,
- working in the world for peace, justice, freedom, and human fulfillment.

❧❧❧❧❧❧❧

I once served as a summer youth worker in a coal camp in Appalachia. I didn't expect the Holiday Inn, but I remember that I was still dumbfounded when breakfast turned out to be a piece of unbuttered toast and a small dab of bacon gravy, without the bacon, in one lonely corner of an otherwise empty plate.

Perhaps that sort of hunger is no worse and no less tragic than the hunger of someone who has silk sheets to sleep between and a Ferrari in the driveway, but has found nothing that has taken possession of life, no mighty dream, no God to trust, no work to do, no love to love, no victory to win, no noble death to die.

❧❧❧❧❧❧❧

Do you remember the resurrection appearance in the Emmaus inn? Jesus had seemed like just another stranger to certain disciples as they journeyed south that first Easter night. But when he took bread, gave thanks, broke it, and gave it to them, their eyes were opened and they recognized him!

Why do we miss seeing him?

We look in the wrong places. In a stained-glass house, perhaps, when he is really looking for us and touching our lives, as Albert Schweitzer put it, "in the toils, the conflicts, and the sufferings we are passing through."

There he is in that child's face or question. In the love of our parents for us, or their patience with our stupidities. In sleep and laughter, in heart attacks and on New Year's Eve, in our daily newspaper, in moments alone under a diamond sky, or one night when we sit and talk late with an understanding friend.

The bread and wine of the Holy Communion—simple food—remind us that he comes to us in events as ordinary as eating, in sexualness, in a walk through the rain. A dandelion flower, a kiss, a fall of snow, a reunion at an airport, a letter in the mail.

> Scattered Christians!
> You out there
> Representing Christ to the world
> On the west side, south side, east side, north side . . .
>
> Scattered Christians!
> You out there
> On your missions for Christ
> In schools, offices, factories, kitchens, open air . . .
>
> Assemble, scattered Christians!
> Assemble at the Holy Table
> Where Christ is host
> And offers you Himself,
> His body in the bread,
> His blood in the wine.
>
> Assemble, scattered Christians!
> Bring your wounded hearts,
> Your aching muscles,
> Your fagged voices,
> Your ragged tempers,
> Your slowed-down brains,
> Your optimism gone sour,
> Your open hands too tired to give again.
>
> Assemble, scattered Christians!
> Tired Christians,
> Worn-out Christians,
> Trying to go it alone.

Assemble at Christ's Table
And feel once again the adrenalin
Of His love
In His Body,
The Church.

Then scatter again, assembled Christians!
Scatter, knowing that you are not alone ever,
And that you are as strong as Christ Himself![6]

Jesus remains in so many ways the stranger who knocks at the door, asking to be a stranger no longer. And we are strangers in Paradise.

This is Paradise. Where you live is Paradise.

Today is Eden.

Life is Eden.

In a world as ambiguous as it is beautiful—a world that excites us to rapture by pink tulips and silver starlight, yet at other times crushes our krispy-cracker defenses by innocent sufferings—in a world where some own his-and-hers Cadillacs while others die because they don't have enough to eat—in a world pluralistic and technologically sophisticated to a fare-you-well, but where many still wonder if there is any difference between right and wrong, and, if so, what the difference is—in such a world and in such an age, Christian courage is another proud and needed witness.

It was a typical blue-gold October afternoon. Activity on the campus was getting up to speed. Term papers were being assigned. Sounds of "hut, hut" and leathery collisions were rising up from the football field. The first big weekend parties had been announced. Life was a four-foot pennant flapping in the academic wind.

In a second-floor room of a freshman dorm, though, Sherry lay stretched out on her stomach. Her face was buried in a tear-wet pillow. She had come with I-can't-wait expectations, a nifty wardrobe, a good mind, a happy smile. But one thing after another had gone wrong. Ready to cut and run, she had written a homesick letter to her parents.

In her college mailbox was an answer to her letter. After a supper that went half eaten, she found it and went off alone to read. It said, in part:

Dear Sherry,

Your letter is one more in a larger series of daily reminders of how much we love you, and of what pride we have in your decision to enroll at State.

Thanks for letting your mother and me know how you are and for leveling about your discouragements. They will pass. Brighter hours will surely take their place. Hang in there, Babe!

Among other thoughts that come and go in your head this first year away from home, I hope you will find a way to remind yourself that, in addition to being a good student, our lovely daughter, and your own unique self, you are also a Christian, and that among the fine strengths of that faith are some, I know, you have made your own. They are there to draw upon in times of both need and great joy.

A verse of the Bible I sometimes turn to in times of trouble is 1 John 5:4: "This is the victory that conquers the world, our faith."

We'll be telephoning soon with family news, and be glad to have you call us too.

We love you fantastically,
Dad

There is also a witness called endurance (Rom. 5:1–5).

There's a formula teachers sometimes recite that bears upon Christian discipleship. It says: "I hear and I forget; I see and I remember; I do and I understand."

Tests reveal we remember only 25 to 30 percent of what we *hear,* 60 or 65 percent of what we *see,* but more than 90 percent of what we *do.*

"Not everyone who says to me, 'Lord, Lord,' will enter the kingdom of heaven, but only the one who does the will of my Father in heaven" (Matt. 7:21). Jesus says that over and over.

He also told a parable about two sons who were asked to work in the vineyard. One said, "Sure, I'll go," but didn't. The second said, "No, I have too many other things to do," but went. In good Socratic fashion, Jesus drove the point home with a question: "Which of the two did the will of his father?"

Suppose we start out on Monday morning, intending to try to live up to such instructions. We have heard the gospel on Sunday. Now we want to *do.* What handles can we grab hold of to authenticate our faith?

Most days we'll get the chance. We'll face some choice, meet some person, find ourselves confronted with an opportunity to act out our love for God. We cannot know, as the sun rises and the day begins, when such moments will come, when the telephone will ring, or what form the summons to our discipleship will take. But we are sure the world out there has needs. It's filled with lonely people, isolated people, hungry people, unfree people. There's evil to be defied; lies to be answered; hate rebuked by love; ugliness outshone by beauty.

And we bear this witness both individually and as One Loaf.

Sometimes the witness signals we send are not the ones we think we are sending or want to be sending at all.

We depend upon words to deliver the freight, but they wind up inadequate and misleading.

We see this parodied when we watch someone shouting frantically, "I'm not upset! Who's upset? You may be upset, but not me!" Tremble, shake, sputter. Or we have a casual conversation—a happenstance meeting with a friend who asks: "How are you?" "Oh, I'm fine!" But tears drop off each syllable like water off a crystal icicle on a winter noon.

We call this *body language.* What our body is saying, what our muscles, our eyes, our hands, and our walk—which are more eloquent than any noisy vocabulary might be—say is, "I didn't sleep well last night." Or, "Somewhere along the way, the excitement of living died inside me." Or, "I'm too busy to listen to you." Or, "I'm anxious, afraid, tense, unable to trust." Or, "I'm in love. I'm open to your entry. My life is rooted in hope."

This is scary. It means we are more naked than we may like to be. But it also assures us that God is imparted through the imperfect humanity of people just like ourselves.

And there is the witness of our dying as, each year, Easter finds us asking for an end to our kidding.

Easter is daybreak. It's children off to church school with envelopes clutched in their hands, symbolizing that unless life is lived for others, there is no life.

It's breakfast on the beach, Peter jumping out of the boat, slogging his way through mist and surf toward shore, unable to believe his eyes. It's the disciples running. Thomas doubting. A fabricated story by the chief priests—a Watergate coverup—that some followers had come by night and stolen the corpse in order to deceive the public.

It is the young church in action, preaching the new life. The warm winds after winter, nests in the front yard. Flower fragrance, and friendship. The color yellow. The end of Lent.

It's telling us that if we're not busy being born, we're busy perishing. Easter is rebirth. It's believing God's creation is constantly in motion, that it's always going somewhere new; and we're hanging on to the side rails, hats flying off as we whip around the corner.

⚞⚟⚞⚟⚞⚟

"If the earthly tent we live in is destroyed," began the apostle Paul in one of his most memorable sentences (2 Cor. 5:1).

Tents are not meant to last forever and not designed to stay in one place.

We enjoy them because they draw us back to land and sky. Their walls are thinner. Through them we can hear the sounds of night; through their seams we catch glimpses of light on even longer journeys than our own.

The first summer after our family moved to California, we decided to visit Yosemite and arranged to stay at one of the tent villages the National Park Service operates there. The tents were clean and snug. Each had a concrete base and was perfect for lying down to sleep with evergreen perfume blessing the air.

As darkness fell, we made up the bunks and our two children lay down inside. Outside were two folding chairs, so Virginia and I, not ready yet for sleeping, decided to sit in front of our little canvas house.

A stranger sauntered by and began a friendly conversation. We admitted it was our first night, so he decided to help us adjust to our new environment.

"Do you have food in the tent?" he said. "It's a good idea not to keep food, because the bears are apt to come around and bother you." He wanted only to be neighborly.

I realized that inside the tent were two pairs of still very wide-awake eyes, and still-listening ears that surely grew wider when they heard these words of warning. A few minutes later came a voice:

"Daddy?"

"Yes?"

"Will the bears come to our tent?"

"No, I don't think so. They may come around the garbage cans around the Lodge, but I feel sure they won't bother us. Besides, there are rangers to protect us."

"Is it all right then to go to sleep?"

"Yes, it is all right to go to sleep."

Death is not a mistake. At times it may seem like the enemy, like a gangster lurking beside the road, ready to rip us off. But God is Lord of death, and these tentative tents given to us to live in for four score and twenty, more or less, years are not oversights but forewords.

Faith, hope, and love are the backpacks we carry, and they are not heavy.

Nor is the dream we lug along with our canteens and K-rations. It doesn't weigh much, either, for it's the dimmest of blueprints.

We can't see the future or draw descriptions of what it will be like, but we can rest in faith that Jesus is in its midst. That's at least part of what the Second Coming is about.

Faith's poetry.

Faith's way of saying that in God's new world, there is neither emptiness nor hate.

Not the end of everything by fire and ice.

Rather, a welcome.

New and bright beginnings.

Chapter 4

Order

Welcome Alternative to Chaos

*O*ne Saturday night on a crowded cable car in San Francisco, I experienced an exhilarating feeling of community I've never forgotten.

It was a mixture of banter, laughter, humor, squeezing, a clanging bell, a good-natured conductor, people of all shapes and ages in rapport with that particular moment.

It seemed like a living parable of what God must have dreamed about at the start.

Life *is* a Saturday-night ride on a cable car, and there are plenty of occasions where order, organization, rules, and procedures are out of place.

At other times they are not only "in place"; but also the welcome and necessary alternative to chaos.

The kingdom is not made primarily out of order any more than a happy home is one where everything is always in its correct, neatly folded location. Disorder, though, is more often an ally of slavery, weakness, and confusion than of true freedom. There's a difference between being really free and being merely unbuttoned; liberation is not license.

Order exists for one rousing reason: to liberate minds and hands for something else.

Sometimes the bureaucratic weight of trying to do the Master's work comes close to crushing our happiness in finding him in the first place. We wallow in the midst of a paper storm. Still, order is as necessary to the gaining of good results in the church as messy politics are in the exercise of democracy.

Our goal should be to let order serve us, and not the other way around.

⌇⌇⌇⌇⌇⌇⌇

A missionary to Japan and a Japanese Christian were making an all-day journey over a mountain to a village on the other side. They carried their food on their backs. At noon they sat by the trail and ate, and the Japanese Christian made this remark: "As long as our food was outside of ourselves it was a burden to be carried. Now that it is inside it becomes a source of power and strength." Faith, when it is too much outward paraphernalia, can also be a problem; but when it is an inward set of the soul, it is the supreme adventure.

⌇⌇⌇⌇⌇⌇⌇

Edward O'Rear, age ninety-six, sat on a porch drenched in gold Kentucky sunshine. He stroked the head of a lovely shepherd dog stretched out beside his chair and looked off in the direction of a tender stand of dogwood trees.

I was a young minister, just arrived in the bluegrass to begin work, and I had been told Judge O'Rear could brief me about a lot of things I ought to know about living among and working with some of eastern Kentucky's mountaineers.

Now he was speaking. "My father and I together," he said, "have lived under every president of the United States from Washington on." Never before had I been so conscious of the adolescence of America.

Later, when a tour guide in Rome reminded me that an old walled town was already eight hundred years old when Jesus was born at Bethlehem, I would have the same feeling all over again.

Actually, it is but four or five lifetimes ago that John Witherspoon, president of the College of New Jersey and moderator of our first General Assembly, signed his name to the Declaration of Independence—a daring act that gave rise to the saying in England that "Cousin America has run off with a Presbyterian parson!"

In colonial America, the war of revolution was referred to as "the Presbyterian rebellion."

If, in our imaginary time machine, we crank in two hundred more years, we are back to Calvin of Geneva. And we notice that he has a pen in his hand.

He's writing what will become known as the *Institutes of the Christian Religion,* the first systematic statement of reformed Christianity (1536). He had reluctantly reached the conclusion that the church as it had come to exist in the sixteenth century was too corrupt and alienated from its New Testament origins to save or reclaim, with its system of clerical hierarchy, long pages of saints, worship of Mary, holy places, holy objects, holy vocations, and indulgences for a fee. A new beginning had to be made with the Bible rather than an institution at its center.

Calvin came a few years after Luther. In Scotland, John Knox would build upon Calvin's work in the sixteenth century. And out of the whole reform effort would come a church closer to apostolic thought and practices than the one which, over the thousand years previously, had almost replaced the Man of Galilee and his spontaneous company of followers— like a few white birches overgrown by a rain forest.

Throwing out the mischievous or inept is one thing. Devising a new system that will achieve results is another—one that will preserve the mystery and necessity of the church as the community of the Holy Spirit, but also has built into it protections against abuse. A system was needed that allowed those who read the Bible to obey their own understanding of the Word, to be free, serving Christ only in their conscience, but also tightly bound to one another in holy community, love, and action.

If the people insist that they are mature and wise enough to govern the church themselves, without having it ruled by a pope and bishops, how will they go about it? Sample question: Who will decide who is to hold the pastor-priestly office, if anyone at all? The result: a representative system that will later serve as political model for the founders of the United States of America.

John Calvin was a Frenchman and a lawyer. He had been persuaded by William Farel of Geneva to come to that Swiss city to help the church recover from the trauma brought about by the religious upheaval sweeping all of central and southern Europe.

What happened there is a long story, but one Presbyterians should come to know. If your church library is without some good historical reference books, why not make it your business to see that they are obtained?

Today the World Alliance of Reformed Churches has its international headquarters in Geneva and includes a fascinating array of spiritual communities such as the Presbyterian Church of New Zealand, the Presbyterian Church in Canada, the Presbyterian Church in Grenada, and the Uniting Church in Australia.

Presbyterians have sometimes been identified as humorless and austere, a frozen rather than a chosen people, who imagine God in wrathful, almost frightening terms—a people who care more about *order* than *ardor.*

But that is as distorted as something else Judge O'Rear told me that day. Kentuckians, he said, are stereotyped in two opposite categories. Fifty-one weeks of the year, they are ignorant moonshiners. But, during the first week in May each year, when the Kentucky Derby is run, they all live in white mansions, sit on broad green lawns, and drink mint juleps.

The Calvin seal shows a heart held in an outstretched hand, and anyone who comes to know the Presbyterian Church—to know its people, its priorities, its worship, its joys, and its memories—will also come to know that the yearning to be faithful to Jesus is what gives us our character and direction of march. If our worship of God is marked by awe, it is not because we are afraid of intimacy, but because we are moved by wonder.

❦❦❦❦❦❦❦

We seek the benefits of order through a system of constitutional law.

Eight "Historic Principles of Church Order" stand as an introduction to the Form of Government, one of the principal sections of the *Book of Order,* which dates back to 1788. They set forth key assumptions of our connectional approach to church life and should be studied, especially by officers.

Presbyterians recognize three ordained offices: ministers of the Word and Sacrament, elders, and deacons. All have a biblical basis; all take similar vows. Elders and ministers, acting together as the session, oversee the total good of the church, receive and dismiss members, provide opportunities for spiritual nurture, control the use of physical properties, and represent the congregation in the higher governing bodies.

Deacons lead the ministries of compassion.

Ordination is symbolized by prayers and a laying on of hands. Ministers are ordained by presbyteries, elders and deacons by sessions.

Election and ordination represent not so much the granting of honor as the assumption of responsibility. It has been said that ordination does not mean so much the laying on of hands as it does the *raising* of hands!

Because all churches are now incorporated and corporate

trustees are mandated by law, congregations must also elect and install trustees. The corporation is a modern idea, and, because trustees were unknown in biblical times, we cannot speak of this as an ordained office, but we do regard it as one of special usefulness.

Elders may serve simultaneously as trustees, in which case the arrangement is called *unicameral.* Other congregations use a *bicameral* arrangement, with a separate board of trustees.

The work both of deacons and of trustees is subject to the overall authority of the session.

We sometimes speak of "the minister and the session," but the minister and any associate ministers are *part of* the session. (Not so in the case of assistant ministers.)

The minister holds membership in both the session and the presbytery, but *not* in the congregation. This means that someone representative of the larger fellowship is always present when the session assembles. This arrangement also protects the minister from the threat of local intimidation.

Session discussions and minutes are confidential. If they were not, the ability to speak candidly about important matters would be impaired. An elder needs to be able to cast a vote on a question without having to defend that vote publicly. Authority is, as we have written, corporate and not personal. Yet any member of the congregation, with any reason to be interested in the outcome of a specific matter, will, in nearly all cases, be welcomed and granted the privilege of the floor by the session, although that privilege could be denied.

Sessions owe congregations full, consistent, informative reports on decisions reached; goals; issues the session may be struggling with; what is happening at presbytery, synod, and General Assembly levels; and the imperatives of mission.

Elders need to be sensitive to congregational feelings and opinions, but their first responsibility is to Jesus Christ and their own consciences. This is fundamental within our system. Elders are not called to manage Christ's affairs by applause meters or nose counts. It would also be a denial of our system to instruct the vote of an elder named to represent the congregation at presbytery, or the vote of a presbyter elected as a commissioner to either synod or the General Assembly.

When votes are split, there should not be a sorrowful wringing of hands on the assumption that the seeds of disunity have been sown. Split votes are normal—a sign that elders are paying attention and that they care enough to disagree.

There is usually merit on both sides of important questions. It is probably safe to guess that, where there are *no* divisions, questions that should be asked, aren't.

When an elder attends presbytery in an official capacity, that elder is serving as a presbyter—as an officer and decision maker within the Presbyterian Church—and not simply as one delegated to bring home a report on presbytery's actions.

There may be the feeling, where an elder is chosen as an official delegate from a congregation, that a responsibility exists to represent the particular congregation from which he or she has come. This is partly true. When we are presbyters, we may be the only voice of the congregation that has sent us. But our first calling as presbyters will be to listen to another voice—to seek the kingdom of God and the truth of God above all else.

Not much has been written here of deacons. Yet they are in so many ways the point at which the gospel is practiced at short range and brought to focus. Without such under-shepherds and persons of extraordinary sensitivity and conscience, we might be left in the position of doing little more than talking about ministry to "the least of these," or of spending all our time and energy tying ourselves up in administrative knots but never getting beyond that.

In most congregations, deacons are faithfully at work performing traditional acts of kindness—calling on the sick and the confined in hospitals, retirement homes, and prisons; visiting members; maintaining contacts with military persons and families, students away at school, and students from other places temporarily residing within the parish. They also collect food and distribute emergency aid to assist people whose needs become known. They are busy and do their work well, sometimes joining with the session to raise basic questions about the ministry of the whole congregation or the root causes of poverty and human disorder.

By seeking out members who have special problems and responding to their needs, deacons create networks of sustaining, supporting, compassionate relationships.

Maggie Kuhn, an exemplary Presbyterian activist, once wrote:

> Deprivation is not confined to the inner city or rural slum. People in white suburban ghettos suffer from cultural deprivation and isolation. The church has a mission to discover persons and groups who are estranged, rejected, forgotten by others, or locked into their own private worlds. In our complex urbanized way of life this search is not easy.
>
> As deacons react to community need and deprivation, they are spying out the land "out there" where church members conduct their daily lives. They are trying to discover what is human and just, and what makes human beings fully human. They are observing God's action in the world and attempting to be sensitive to the appropriate response. Having "intelligence" about what is going on in the world, they return to the church to regroup their forces, to be renewed by prayer and worship, to map the strategy that will guide and encourage the Christian community as a whole.[7]

Authority is occasionally demonstrated by a show of strength, more often by knowledge, patience, and love. It is the cement that holds personality together, that enables families, governments, and civilizations to survive.

The lack of authority is as harmful as the exercise of too much, or its wrongful use. An Old Testament book ends on an anarchical and pathetic note: "In those days there was no king in Israel; all the people did what was right in their own eyes" (Judg. 21:25).

For the opposite end of the spectrum, choose any totalitarian system you please, or conjure up the image of a family built on foundations of fear and threats of physical punishments rather than understanding and mutual pride.

Our church seeks to preserve a delicate, pragmatic balance between authority and freedom.

The Presbyterian Church (U.S.A.) is representative and constitutional democracy, and not pure democracy or unlimited majority rule. Dozens of decisions, under our system, are made *not* by the people directly but by the people's representatives.

These decisions include receiving, dismissing, and disciplining members; deciding the nature of programs of Christian education; fixing staff salaries; determining ministries of outreach to be supported by the people's gifts; and selecting those who will represent the congregation at meetings of the presbytery.

The congregation, however, exercises authority in two crucial areas: It decides who the pastor will be (subject to presbytery confirmation) and who will constitute the official boards.

The pastor has a rather limited domain: choosing hymns, Scriptures, and prayers for worship; determining the content of the sermon—important guarantees of a free pulpit.

The preacher is beholden to no one except the Spirit of Christ.

The *Book of Order* defines the role of pastors as being responsible for "studying, teaching, and preaching the Word, for administering Baptism and the Lord's Supper, for praying with and for the congregation."

Presbyteries have authority to ordain ministers, to organize and dissolve congregations, and to discipline pastors and congregations under the *Book of Order.* Pastors are members of a presbytery rather than of a congregation. Wise ministers accept advice from their sessions but can be called to account for their ministries only by the presbytery.

Presbyteries are not autonomous. They are subordinate creations of the General Assembly, as well as, collectively, the Assembly's creators.

Synods have limited authority but make it possible for presbyteries and Presbyterians to engage in regional strategies and fellowship.

So the church functions, as does the country, interdependently—with nerves, spine, ligaments, and brain seeking the harmony of movement that will produce forward movement toward a City of Truth.

This seems to require a jillion rules—committees, commissions, councils, task forces, reports, and overtures, and a ceaseless striving to see that all things are done "decently and in order" (1 Cor. 14:40), creating a weight that at times makes it seem we are not an Easter people at all, but a huge wallowing whale—a vast, narcissistic corporation, the Savior nowhere in sight.

Yet the system works, and everyone who has ever attended a General Assembly, either as an elected commissioner or simply as an observer, gasps in amazement that so many can sit down and do Christ's business together and leave as friends.

We occasionally hear it said, "Presbytery is the bishop."

This is more than a cliché. We have no district superinten-
dents, no bishops or archbishops. We have only ourselves,
our rules, our respect for one another, and Jesus Christ. We
also have a system that appropriates the guidance of a well-
educated clergy, and the guidance of lay women, men, and
youth who share on equal terms in deciding what the gospel
is in and for our own time, and how we can best go about its
implementation.

Overtures (they originate at either the session or presbytery level) are petitions that, in most cases, call upon the
church as a whole to amend its position or law, change a
boundary, send a message of social concern, or initiate action
that affects this organism we call the body of Christ.

Once overtures reach the Assembly, they are evaluated.
That body decides whether to refer the proposals involved to
the presbyteries for voting.

Overtures amending the *Book of Order* require a majority
vote of the presbyteries; those that seek to change the *Book
of Confessions* require a two-thirds vote and ratification by a
subsequent General Assembly.

Overtures are not voted on directly by congregations. To
more than a few Presbyterians, this is a puzzlement. If we had
a congregational-type government, we would vote this way.
We are consistent in putting trust not in individuals but in representative bodies. We not only elect them; we also empower
them to act.

There is risk in such a process, but strength too.

❦❦❦❦❦❦❦

A few significant facts:

- The first General Assembly met in Philadelphia in 1789,
  the same year that the American Constitution was
  adopted. It meets annually in various sections of the
  country, though, after 2005, it will begin meeting every
  other year.

- The moderator, elected by the commissioners at the Assembly's opening, may be a pastor or an elder. She or he serves for one year without salary and travels throughout the church, visiting various points of mission at home and abroad to symbolize its unity and help give direction and inspiration to its work.
- Each General Assembly brings together about five hundred commissioners, elected by the presbyteries on a pro rata basis (according to the number of members) and in such numbers as to ensure a fifty-fifty balance between elders and ministers. Ordinarily, it lasts eight days and transacts an enormous amount of business. There are reports from the church's many agencies and departments, plus reports by special task forces and the Permanent Judicial Commission (see glossary). The Assembly also makes decisions on dozens of overtures—referring some back to the presbyteries for corporate vote and rejecting others altogether.
- Minutes of the General Assembly are a valuable resource for learning about the overall life of the Presbyterian Church. One volume contains statistics compiled from annual reports submitted by the constituent congregations; the other is a journal summarizing all the Assembly's actions and reproducing the major reports presented.
- The Stated Clerk of the General Assembly is the continuing executive officer and is elected for a five-year term. The Clerk may be either an elder or a minister.
- The General Assembly of the Presbyterian Church has been described as one of "the great administrative bodies of the Western world." However, if you were to watch some of its meetings, with dozens of commissioners asking for the floor at the same moment, you might be inclined to wonder about the feasibility of that many human beings sitting down to business at the same time.

One of the tenets of Presbyterian theology is the sharing of ministry—the belief that ministry is not something given to a religious elite but to the whole people of God. We think of ourselves as all being ordained to serve, to teach, to pray, and to witness—to be the life of Jesus re-created, relived, and reenacted in our time.

It is not, in our tradition, the pastor who is in the center, but the congregation. It is we—together—who are asked to be the light of the world, the salt, the leaven, the balm of Gilead, the resurrection presence. And none of us can be that alone. We need each other's help in understanding the Bible, even in knowing who we ourselves are. Together, we are children of light and the children of hope because of Jesus Christ.

Contemporary American society has a strangely individualistic note about it. Oh, we have the greatest system of mass communications the world has ever known, but one of the greatest kinds of solitariness the world has known or could ever know would also be a man or woman sitting in front of a machine typing in messages, or absorbing from a video screen an array of material images.

That statement is not intended to be antitechnology; technology is neutral. It can be and will be what we make of it. But we must make some dreams to go along with our new skills. And the electronic church, for all the good things that could and should be said about what it can mean to people's lives, may wind up atomizing them, encapsulating them—not making them whole, but making them more separate.

The enemy is not television, or computers, or the twenty-first century. The enemy is isolation and the fear and the pain that go with being forced to deal with the world on one's own, with only one's own well-being in mind. Is there any way to define love in the singular?

Sometimes a minister has to stand beside people who are

going through times of crisis, asking questions for which there seem to be no believable or satisfying answers. And for many of the things that occur in life, there *is* no explanation. The Bible makes that clear in more than one way and in more than one place.

But we can love and trust, and we can hope even without these longed-for explanations. I like to remind people that, for some of our questions, God has given us not answers but something better than answers: God has given us one another.

"People who need people are the luckiest people in the world," says a popular song. And that's not just a secular fact; it is the gospel. It is God's message to the church. Maybe it helps us to know why life is implicitly incomplete and why none of us has been designed or created to be proudly self-sufficient.

God has come to us in Christ, and Christ comes to us in the church. For all its faults, the church is where many of us met Christ and where we have been permitted to grow in our knowledge and love of him. Whoever is in Christ is a new creation.

The signals that came back from Pioneer X on its trip around Jupiter were so faint, we are told, when it reached the outermost limits of its journey, that these impulses, if collected for nineteen million years, could light a 7½-watt Christmas tree bulb for only 1/1000th of a second.

We, too, have only glimpses to go on, but these are sufficient to wipe out our fears and to keep us pressing on toward a distant City.

Chapter 5

Discipline

The Servant of Mission

*T*he island of Maui is a beautiful place for a vacation. The winds of the Pacific are soft and steady, the sea a blissful blue, the bougainvillea a blaze of red. Cloud-wreathed Haleakala, an old volcanic furnace, now dormant, rises ten thousand feet in the center of this magic fragment of terra firma, which Charles A. Lindbergh said "appears offered to sky by water and pressed to earth by stars."

This apartment we've leased for a two-week's stay also has a small balcony for drinking in the elixirs of first morning and the glamor of the tropical night.

Next door, though, a family vacation quarrel is going on. Voices are rising. There are shouts of "You shut up!" "That isn't fair!" There are threats, anger, crying. A father, trying to make peace among his children, winds up in a rage of his own.

Those same sounds, and the problem of getting along together, are also found sometimes in the church.

That shouldn't surprise us or make us feel hypocritical or apologetic, as if strong emotion—some of it negative—has no place in the affairs of the people of the Way. Politics and religion both arouse subterranean feelings in human beings for an understandable reason: because they deal with such crucial matters as truth, justice, freedom, dignity, credibility, mortality, happiness, and hope.

The Presbyterian system for resolving conflict, and for seeing to it that persons are dealt with fairly in the internal life of the church, is called *discipline.* In fact, one of the sections of the *Book of Order* is called Rules of Discipline.

The average church member is least aware of that part of our government, but we don't spend much time reading and rereading the American Constitution, either. Yet we know its guarantees of protections and rights are there to be called upon when we need them.

☙☙☙☙☙☙☙

John Calvin included discipline as one of the identifying marks of the church of Jesus Christ. The faithful preaching of the gospel and the celebration of the sacraments of baptism and the Lord's Supper were the other two.

Discipline is strength.

It eradicates confusion, minimizes injustice.

It prevents controlling majorities from ignoring unpopular minorities.

Part of our discipline is a reflection of *Robert's Rules of Order,* which are parliamentary rules now used to regulate the business of sessions, presbyteries, synods, and the General Assembly.

☙☙☙☙☙☙☙

A hundred years ago it was common for a church member to be called before the session to explain misbehavior and to be censured for it, or to account for failure to live up to a membership promise.

Today the most vivid encounter many have with the church in its disciplinary role is finding a letter in the mail informing the recipient that a record of consistent inactivity has necessitated either transfer to inactive status or deletion of the person's name altogether from the roll of members.

Members transferred to the inactive roll who remain in that status for two years (nonresidents for one year) are subject to having their names deleted from the membership rolls if there is no evidence of renewed involvement.

Membership doesn't define an organization we belong to. It is, rather, something *we are.*

Ordinarily, sessions do not take removal or erasure actions if any life at all is left in the relationship—if the person involved is making any effort to practice the means of grace: corporate worship, study of the Bible, service to others—the regular exercising of faith that keeps it strong.

⚜⚜⚜⚜⚜⚜⚜

The *Book of Order* has provisions for dealing with almost every conflict that might arise. Although it is not a terribly inspiring piece of literature, it keeps us from flying off centrifugally into space in a hundred jagged pieces when trouble rears its head.

Discipline is the servant of mission.

And the friend of sacrifice.

In spite of its negative, woodshed kind of sound, discipline is part of a *positive* obedience to Jesus Christ.

It manifests itself as courage and as choice.

It is Jesus talking to us about counting the cost.

It is order within worship—not for order's sake, but so whim doesn't take over.

It is the Theological Declaration of Barmen (included in the *Book of Confessions),* whose banner shows the cross of Christ overpowering the swastika of the Third Reich.

It is elders and deacons responding to nine constitutional questions—the favorite seeming to be question eight, "Will you seek to serve the people with energy, intelligence, imagination, and love?"

It is the proportionate dedication of our money to the work of Christ in the world.

It is making ethical choices, studying our marching orders, learning to be disciplined disciples.

It means taking seriously our biblical heritage represented by the *Book of Confessions,* that unfinished symphony of brass, woodwinds, drums, and strings that forms the theological continuum of the living church.

It is the session, sitting down to work and staying until midnight.

It is praying, and continuing to pray, even while the sky is falling on our heads.

Discipline is a substitute for the pastoral prima donna, causing *shared* ministry to come alive—a reminder that the church isn't built on the pluses or minuses of a pastor's personality, but on a covenant to work together as the *ecclesia* even when the congregation may be without a pastor.

Our Constitution describes discipline as an expression of the power Jesus Christ has vested in his church and says it is derived from the Scriptures "for the instruction, training, and correction of its members, officers, congregations, and governing bodies."

It is the spiritual compact of our familyhood, and another evidence that liberty and integrity come through a church of laws.

David Anderson, a Presbyterian pastor in Paisley, Scotland, before emigrating to the United States in 1974, introduced me to these playful lines (original source unknown), which are shared, with an apology for failure to amend the sexist language. Substituting "churchperson" seemed destined to ruin the poem.

> Ten little churchmen went to church when things were
>   fine—
> The going got a little rough—and then there were nine.
>
> Nine little churchmen stayed up very late—
> One slept the Sunday morning through—and then there
>   were eight.

Eight little churchmen on the road to heaven—
One joined the golf club—and then there were seven.

Seven little churchmen solid as the very bricks—
One was asked to serve on session—and then there were
    six.

Six little churchmen kept the place alive—
One liked to watch football games—and then there were
    five.

Five little churchmen seemed loyal to the core—
The sermon offended one—and then there were four.

Four little churchmen argued heatedly
Over church policy—and then there were three.

Three little churchmen sang the service through—
Got a hymn they didn't like—and then there were two.

Two little churchmen disputed who should run
The next church dinner—and then there was one.

One little churchman, wondering what to do,
Brought a friend to church one day—and then there
    were two.

Two sincere churchmen each brought in one more
So their number doubled—and then there were four.

Four sturdy churchmen simply couldn't wait
'Til they found four others—and then there were eight.

Eight eager churchmen at worship every week
Soon encouraged others, troubled souls to seek.

The seats in church were filled with people cramming
    every pew—
May God supply such zeal and love in this church too.

There are in the United States other groups of Christians who either use a presbyterian form of government or the name Presbyterian—such as the Cumberland Presbyterian Church or the Associate Reformed Presbyterian Church. We cooperate with some of these in united expressions of mission.

The Constitution of the Presbyterian Church (U.S.A.) consists of the *Book of Confessions* and the *Book of Order.*

The *Book of Confessions* contains:

> The Nicene and the Apostles' Creeds
> —second to fourth centuries
>
> The Scots Confession, the Heidelberg Catechism (German), the Second Helvetic Confession (Swiss), the Westminster Confession of Faith, the Shorter and Larger Catechisms
> —early Reformation period, sixteenth and seventeenth centuries
>
> The Theological Declaration of Barmen
> —1934, in the face of Nazism, with its barbaric abuses of freedom and human life and attack upon Christianity and the church
>
> The Confession of 1967
> —1967
>
> A Brief Statement of Faith—Presbyterian Church (U.S.A.)
> —1983

These documents help us to know our theological past and present. Together they constitute important references for our growth in faith.

Each contains particular meanings for a particular time (some sound amusingly quaint today), plus meanings that transcend all times and help us appreciate the truth that "Jesus Christ is the same yesterday and today and forever" (Heb. 13:8).

Church members do not formally subscribe to these statements, but they take them seriously because the church does.

Officers promise, at the time of their ordination, to study the confessions and to be guided by them, as well as by the Scriptures, as a discipline of leadership.

The Confession of 1967, because it is more recent, and because it can be read with understanding in about twenty minutes, tends to receive proportionately more attention than the other statements. Quite a few congregations also use parts of it in public worship.

It has a strong central theme: *reconciliation.*

Part I of "C-67" describes God's ministry of reconciliation to us in Jesus Christ.

Part II is a "therefore" follow-up piece to Part I. *Because of* God's reconciling work on our behalf, we believe ourselves sent into the world with a reconciliation ministry of our own. We seek, as representatives of the Christ, to break down hostile barriers that divide persons, races, and nations.

Part III is a brief but needed reminder that, whereas the *fulfillment* of reconciliation probably is not realizable within historical time, it will be realized in the supratemporal concern of the God whose love is forever.

One day I met a friend on the street—a woman who I knew belonged to the Episcopal Church. I asked what she thought of certain ecumenical discussions under way at the time. These discussions, if successful, would produce a union between her denomination and mine. I will never forget her answer. It went like this: "No! I *like* being an Episcopalian. I *enjoy* being an Episcopalian. I want to *die* a member of the Episcopal Church. No! I am totally opposed!"

Differences in forms of worship, systems of government,

and theological understanding are not bad. They are not even unfortunate, so long as they do not estrange people or bring discredit to the truth that we are one in Christ Jesus.

Differences keep life interesting, the church on its toes.

Here are a few distinctive shapes, styles, and stances that might cause some people to say they *like* being Presbyterians (no order of priority intended):

Most Presbyterian congregations prefer a certain majesty and order in their services of worship. Innovation is in, but reverence and a spirit of adoration aren't out.

We do not own the Celtic cross (circle superimposed over cross bars), but, because of its prominence in Scotland, where the moderator's flag still flies over Edinburgh while the General Assembly is meeting, we demonstrate a preference for it.

Presbyterian Women's organizations, by the energy and quality of their programs, exemplary stewardship, triennial assemblies, and publications, impart stature to the church as a whole.

Ghost Ranch and Plaza Resolana (New Mexico), Montreat (North Carolina), and Stony Point (New York)—our three national conference centers—keep the Presbyterian Church relaxed and its intellectual adrenalin flowing.

Presbyterians have always put a high premium on education. They have strongly supported the nation's public schools and warned against allowing them to become second-rate. They pioneered the founding of some of our best liberal arts colleges and have insisted on high standards in theological learning. Candidates for the ordained ministry must pass national standard examinations as well as be graduates of accredited seminaries.

The office of elder epitomizes the best meanings of Presbyterian theology. It makes possible a church set firmly upon the foundation of the priesthood of all believers. Laypersons make fine theologians, evangelists, teachers, and ministers of grace. They show great skill in forming and communicating the church's corporate witness. One visit to a General Assembly will prove it.

And Presbyterians have long been in the forefront of the ecumenical movement, furnishing leaders and dollars. We are related *denominationally* to both the National and World Councils of Churches. We place the interests and needs of the whole household of faith, and of the world community, ahead of denominational and national ones.

We have made love and justice synonymous and indivisible in their claim upon our attention and financial resources.

Although the church school has undergone many changes since its beginnings in England (for underprivileged children) in the late eighteenth century, good teaching and curricula are of maximum importance.

The Mission Yearbook for Prayer and Study represents another yoking: the inward journey of the heart, including intercessory prayer (on behalf of others), combined with the outward journey—deeds of compassion, of healing, helping, and announcing the news of salvation throughout the whole inhabited earth.

⌇⌇⌇⌇⌇⌇⌇

A book of Ray Bradbury plays contains a preface that says they were written to be performed by "any glad company of fools."

That's not a bad name for the church.

We can always meet life with a laugh. The clown has bereft moments, too, and Jesus Christ does not call upon us to whistle our way through the world while people starve and the innocent die in senseless crimes.

But we remain a *glad* people who, even in the presence of some serious disappointments, take our places together regularly in worship and proclaim:

> We do not know what grief or care
> The day may bring;

The heart [that finds] some gladness there ...
Can always sing.[8]

And we are a *glad company.*

The word is singular. We are one in the Spirit, one in the Lord.

We do not all have the same problems. We are not all of the same age. We do not all have the same size family, the same politics, the same amount of money, the same interests, the same color eyes.

But we are one!

The company of the committed, united in and for Jesus Christ.

We suffer together, celebrate one another's triumphs, weep at one another's grief.

Our polity is connectional; so are our hearts.

We emphasize the one, holy, catholic church referred to in the Apostles' Creed, and understand the mission of Jesus as being one enterprise. If the church is in trouble in Korea or Central America, it is *our own body* that is being bruised. If those who direct mission from our national offices shout, "Help! The mission is in trouble," it is to us, who have designed this mission and made it our own, that those words speak and burn their way into our personal and congregational priorities and budgets.

The church is not weakened by diversity, only by division; not by hard debate, but by a failure of gladness.

Who wants to be called a fool? A fool is a sap, an easy mark.
But we are fools for Christ's sake.
Not just fools.
Fools for him.

Chapter 6

Covenant

Promises, Promises

Stewart Alsop was a journalist—one of the fourth estate's best until his death from cancer in the early 1970s.

One night, on a television interview show, he shared with a large national audience a dream he had had in the hospital a couple of months before. In his mixture of dream and vision, he said the hospital had seemed to turn into a train. A conductor was going up and down the aisles calling out, "This train stops at Baltimore!"

Alsop said he arose from his bed, frightened. Something about the conductor's cry was telling him the end of his life was at hand.

Clenching his fists and raising his eyes upward, he shouted back: "This train doesn't stop at Baltimore! This train doesn't stop at Baltimore!" Then he staggered back to bed.

When the dream resumed, he told his audience, the train roared through the Baltimore station without stopping.

Faith is predicated upon a similar view of life.

It is life that will not take credit for itself.

Will not believe that sorrow or evil ever has the final word.

It is Life, grounded in the confidence of covenant.

A *covenant* is a promise or a set of promises given binding authority by some written evidence, seal, or act.

It is a vow to do something or remain loyal to someone.

In law, it carries the force of a contract.

For faith, it rests upon a self-established promise of a Creator-Redeemer God, revealed in Jesus Christ, and confirmed to us by the coming of the Holy Spirit.

Covenant is the Bible's way of describing God's absolute faithfulness.

In such poignant stories as Noah and the ark, Abraham and Isaac, the prophets lifting up voices of hope in the midst of despair, and, most eloquently, in Jesus, who said his death for the sins of all would constitute a new covenant between God and the world, this idea of a kept agreement has turned otherwise fearful men and women into giants.

Covenant theology is our reflection upon the responsibilities involved in keeping such promises and what happens when covenant is broken.

Faith in Jesus creates the covenant community, and baptism with water is the event that salutes our entrance into the joys and expectations of that camaraderie.

Life within the covenant includes all the sheltering, suffering, beauty, identity, forgiveness, and fun that family membership represents.

Children of believers may be baptized even though they are not yet old enough to articulate a faith of their own. *Because the covenant already enfolds them,* it has already begun to shape who and whose they are.

Dick Avery and Don Marsh taught us to sing:

> We are rescued, we are claimed,
> We are loved and we are named.
> We are baptized! . . .
> We have passed thru the waters
> And that's all that matters . . .
> O thanks be to God![9]

Baptism may be deferred, by present church practice, until an age of personal decision.

For children, baptism is not the event that *makes* them Christian. It is the privilege they and their parents enjoy because God has already by virtue of their parents' love and faith encircled them within the wonder of covenant.

ᛤᛤᛤᛤᛤᛤ

God keeps promises. Sometimes we don't. And we see the fruit of our disobedience in social upheaval and personal regret.

When we forget God and say, "My power and the might of my own hand have gotten me this wealth" (Deut. 8:17), we break the bond.

When we pursue our own security, regardless of how it affects the rest of humanity, our souls start to die, our side of the covenant starts to fade.

But God hangs in—

> Man won't come right!
> After your patient centuries,
> Fresh starts, recastings, tired Gethsemanes
> And tense Golgothas, he, your central theme,
> Is just a jangling echo of your dream.
> Grand as the rest may be, he ruins it.
> Why don't you quit?
> . . . .
> Dear God, how you must love your job![10]

At the Rancho Park golf course in West Los Angeles, there's a plaque near one hole. It tells how Arnold Palmer once took twelve shots to get the ball into the cup.

Twelve!

Over the green. Another pitch. This time into sand. So forth; so on. The plaque includes a diagram mapping out each of the shots and telling where each went.

It is so with us. We seek the good. Aim high. Establish our covenants with excellence. Demand integrity and honest performances by those with whom we are involved in business affairs or those who hold public office. Sooner or later, though, we all meet at the foot of the cross in need of mercy, finding our hope in the steadfastness of God rather than in the improvability of humanity.

In 2 Corinthians, Paul writes, "Thanks be to God, who in Christ always leads us in triumphal procession, and through us spreads in every place the fragrance that comes from knowing him" (2 Cor. 2:14).

I was twenty-one and a first-year student at Northwestern's law school in Chicago. I had grown up in a small town, and the Windy City looked very big to me. It was big! Especially impressive were the subway and elevated trains that came down from the North Shore and up from the South Side and circled the heart of the city, to form a loop.

To reach the Loop from the campus, you could ride on either the subway or the above-ground El. I chose the El because it passed Holloway's candy factory. What you could inhale from the train on a summer afternoon, when the train's windows were open, was something!

The Christian life is like a trip past Holloway's. A wind is blowing fragrance against our faces, countering the pollutions that make us wonder where the perfume of life has gone.

We are in covenant with a world God both created and cares about. The razing of barriers between sacred and secular was part of the mission of Jesus, and continues to be nonnegotiable in Presbyterian thought.

We hold that God loves the world and believes in it; that neither prayer, nor worship, nor radical trust amounts to a separate realm for "hiding from it." Faith is embrace, not escape.

We meet God in our play as well as in our prayers, on our freeways as well as on the road to Jericho, at our office desks as well as around the table in the upper room. Jesus would be disappointed if we tried to have it any other way.

Some write off the world as hopeless. They present faith as an option to keep the world from getting to you. It is distorted into a call to avoid life. Divide soul from body, the service of worship from the welfare rolls.

Presbyterians stand against such separation and call it sinful.

The Holy Spirit, God's active, omnipresent love, is our reminder of covenant.

The Holy Spirit is more than a stir of emotional breezes. The Spirit is also a wind for driving ships, for creating the Easter life out of the dust of August.

As Christian disciples, we also honor a covenant of listening. In a sound-saturated society like ours, listening tends to be a lost art.

Presbyterians believe God and one may be a majority. At the same time we affirm that possibility, we also affirm the importance of studying God's Word to guide our judgment, and of listening to one another in love.

We reject a private Christianity.

The right and duty to obey conscience is inextricably linked to a companion belief that the robe of Christ is without seam.

We are in covenant, not only with Christ, but also with one another.

The Bible is covenant theater, presented in three acts, bracketed by a prologue and an epilogue.

In any good story, the stage must first be set.

In old-time films, Western sagas were usually introduced with a few rolling paragraphs that explained the year and place—Dodge City, 1895—plus a few comments about the times and the kinds of crises persons were living with then.

The Bible presents, in the first eleven chapters of Genesis, the problem, the situation. If we were to assign this first part of the Scriptures a title, it might read: "Here Is What God Was Up Against."

In these chapters, persons are seen as made in the image of God but living in separation from God as a result of their own choice. In these first chapters is a profound ancient account of the divine beginnings of humanity and life, the dawning of the human spirit.

Here, in story form, are some first efforts to answer questions like: Why two sexes, male and female? What do the lives of men and women have to do with one another? Why do people feel a need to hide their bodies? Why do people speak different languages? How did evil get into the world? How did things get to be the way they are?

Most importantly, we have in this magnificent introduction a picture of humankind, created for responsible relationships but living in alienation. That is why the story that follows is necessary.

ᎦᎦᎦᎦᎦᎦᎦᎦ

Act 1 tells how God delivered the Hebrews from Egyptian bondage; more specifically, from capture by Pharaoh at the Red Sea. It begins at Genesis 12, where as a people we make an entrance onto the stage of recorded history around 1900 B.C. with the call of Abraham. We are concerned with Abraham because his considerable number of descendants from twelve great-grandsons and their progeny become, as the result of a famine at home, slaves in Egypt. At first they are "in," for their brother is Joseph, who holds high office in government. But then comes, in Exodus 1:8, an unsettling sentence: "Now a new king arose over Egypt, who did not know Joseph."

Some four hundred years transpire between the poignant tale of Joseph and his brothers and this negative turn of events. By this time, instead of twelve brothers, Abraham's family numbers in the thousands. Suddenly, they find themselves servants of the Egyptians.

Then comes escape, the parting of waters, which the Hebrews (Abraham's people) understand as God's miraculous intervention on their behalf. Next come forty years of wandering in the wilderness behind Moses, during which time the people receive the Ten Commandments and other forms of divine help. Finally, dignity and freedom and prosperity are restored in the land from which the Hebrews had come generations before.

Act 1 ends here.

All the first part of the Old Testament turns on this event—deliverance and rescue from slavery. The pages literally shout: *God acts in history! God does great deeds!*

Act 2 is a story about exile.

This act is different from the wilderness experience.

It begins with the Israelites settled in the promised land, reaching their zenith about 1000 B.C. under David. But storm clouds are building in the east. Triumph turns into a story of national decline, prophetic warnings, a charge that the nation has forgotten God, a crisis of belief, and political division.

In 587 B.C., one of the most significant dates of biblical history, we witness the collapse of Judah. Jerusalem's Temple is destroyed, and it's back to the salt mines of oppression for those people who insist on calling themselves God's elect. This time Babylon is the conqueror. This second bondage lasts seventy years. In Isaiah and in Psalm 137 we hear sounds of crying and homesickness.

This is interrupted by the promise of another deliverance and a Deliverer. One undefeated man, a remembering Jew, clings to hope. "Be comforted, my people," he proclaims. "God will soon let you return home. God will build a highway across the desert, and we will go back to our beloved Jerusalem."

The people do return, some at least. But everything has changed.

Ezra and Nehemiah describe the problems the Hebrews faced in trying to rebuild the Temple and reestablish the old way of life.

The community is re-formed, but the fires of faith burn low. During this stage the psalms are collected and made into the hymnbook of the rebuilt Temple.

The writing we know as the book of Jonah appears during this time as a rebuke to the narrowness of these people returning home, and to their lack of any real compassion for the people who live around them. Jonah reluctantly goes to Nineveh to preach the love of God after his attempts to run away fail. The people to whom he preaches repent and believe. Jonah sulks! He discovers he can more easily believe God loves him than believe that God loves all persons. The book of Jonah blasts the narrow and nationalistic spirit of his people.

Act 2 ends in a whimpering, pessimistic darkness, with talk of a Messiah who will come. But the talk grows fainter and fainter—and finally dies off into silence on the night winds, interrupted in the last two centuries before Christ only by the Maccabean struggles and rhythmical boot steps of Roman legions.

Act 3 opens with an orchestra playing softly.

A man and a woman make their way from Nazareth to Bethlehem for the tax-record enrollment ordered by Caesar Augustus for all his puppet provinces. Then the music swells in a crescendo as the Son of God dies on the cross at the hands of a mob.

Now the audience is in tears. The failure of humanity that began in Genesis—Abel's murder, the chaos of Babel— seems unchanged and unrelieved. Although the life of Jesus looks at first like a triumph on God's part, suddenly at the cross that triumph becomes Dunkirk!

Then, just as the play seems to have taken a hopeless and

irreparable turn, the appearance of the risen Christ among dispirited followers renews the broken talk of God and humankind.

Act 3, the coming of Jesus as the Christ, tells us God still walks the roads of history.

A new Israel emerges. The new Israel is the church, whose origins are chronicled in Acts and in the collected correspondence of those first believers and their leaders.

Greenness begins to spread across the earth again in testimony to the fact that God is still there, that God *will* prevail, will never give up. Such is the gospel. "If we are faithless, he remains faithful—for he cannot deny himself" (2 Tim. 2:13).

The Old Testament tells us God is power as well as love; the New Testament tells us God is love as well as power. Power and love spell hope.

As the Bible has a prologue, it also has an epilogue, the book of Revelation. This closing book of the Bible, through elaborate symbolism, tells us two things:

First, we learn that the war between God and Satan, between the grandeur and wretchedness of humanity, continues.

Second, the ultimate result is not in doubt. God will win. In Jesus Christ, God has already won the victory. John, writing from Patmos, closes with words of radiant invitation: "And let everyone who is thirsty come. Let anyone who wishes take the water of life as a gift" (Rev. 22:17).

We leave the theater, realizing we have not only witnessed a performance but also caught a glimpse of ourselves upon this stage.

We know we have more to do now than just stop off for a late night refreshment before going home to bed. God has nailed us with this story. We cannot go back to where we were.

Maybe we wonder if we should have gone to the theater in the first place.

But we did. And life will never be the same.

In the Hawaiian Islands sunrise and sunset are glorious moments indeed, purple and gold spectaculars, cloud castles and flaming arrows.

That's true, though, everywhere.

Kate Kelley once remarked as we were driving to a meeting of presbytery in Iowa: "November sunsets are the dividends the year pays before it closes its books."

Select *any* second of *any* day or night. At precisely that instant, somewhere on earth's surface it is the moment for those "first rose-gold points of sunrise." At another, for the pressed lips of sunset.

It's *always* sunrise and *always* sunset—somewhere.

It is where we stand, sit, or lie to watch that makes the difference.

Even when we are not present, it is sunrise and sunset in those places—that continual birthing and expiring that give us a sense of time.

It makes the same difference depending upon the position we choose from which to measure or contemplate the church. Or the human story in general.

There's always discouraging information to which we may turn: the threat of nuclear annihilation. The seeming incapacity of the planet, with its diminishing resources and rising populations, to satisfy tomorrow. Our fumbling experimentation with obituaries and revivals of religion. The disarray of the American family. Sunset. Shadows.

But there are signs of hope, too. Equal opportunity for all persons is *beginning* to become a fact. There's a new consciousness of interdependency among nation-states, an awakening to the urgencies of world hunger. Quarreling between generations so prominent during the sixties is being laid aside. (Who gets upset about long hair styles any longer?) Statistical charts for the organized church have begun to flatten out. Freshness has entered worship. The fire of an informed, passionate evangelism has been rekindled. Sunrise. Morning glories. Signs of a new and better day.

Even without proof of renewal, we can still rejoice. Even in the darkness, we can still believe in the light. That is what covenant faith is about. It's as indestructible as the promise it trusts in.

Whatever may be wrong about us who call ourselves Presbyterians, this much has to be right: We know how to face the future unafraid.

> There are two majorities, son, though you ask me no question. The nameless dead, the unborn legions of time, but we are the thin minority, the living, who hold God's sceptre of light.[11]

Sometimes we find ourselves mentally reliving the bubbly optimism of the Kennedy years. The world seemed young then. We felt idealistic. We were convinced we stood on some undeniable and undenying threshold of greatness. Then assassination. War. Shortages. Suddenly we were wretched and old and dying. We seemed to enter the winter of the human spirit.

Both extremes are just that—distant ends on the hope scale. Near the middle, life goes on. A song can still be heard. A few still dream and dance the dance of life. God's love has not lost its power, nor prophetic anger its usefulness in keeping us advancing along the pathway of our own Pilgrim's Progress.

Someone said not long ago that we no longer understand history in terms of its ascendancy. I can't get that statement out of mind. It is true, and by being true it is both honest and dangerous.

The time has come for us to face up to the practical limits of our sphere, the perishability of the environment, the need for a responsible stewardship of land, sea, and air if earth is to be habitable for anyone fifty years from now. We can't use and use, spend and spend, consume and litter indefinitely. To do so is both bad economics and contemptible morality.

But we must not be so obsessed with the ethics of survival that we neglect another form of ethics—the ethics of hope, the promise and guarantee that all things are possible with God.

It isn't autumn for the human spirit; it's spring.

Forever spring somewhere, just as it's forever sunrise somewhere—anywhere and everywhere that the church refuses to give up its franchise of hope.

When Christians hope, they are already beginning to change life for the better. They are doing more than yearning.

They are living out a reality.

"A Declaration of Faith," prepared by the Presbyterian Church U.S. prior to the 1983 Reunion, reads in part:

> In Christ God gave us a glimpse of the new creation he has already begun and will surely finish.
>
> We do not know when the final day will come.
>
> In our time we see only broken and scattered signs that the renewal of all things is under way.
>
> We do not yet see the end of cruelty and suffering in the world, the church, or our own lives.
>
> But we see Jesus as Lord.
>
> As he stands at the center of our history, we are confident he will stand at its end.
>
> He will judge all people and nations.
>
> Evil will be condemned and rooted out of God's good creation.
>
> There will be no more tears or pain.
>
> All things will be made new.
>
> The fellowship of human beings with God and each other will be perfected.[12]

Chapter 7

A Presbyterian Glossary

*H*ere are some terms Presbyterians use in their common life and work:

Assistant/Associate pastor
Assistant pastors are invited by sessions. Associate pastors are called by congregations.

Book of Common Worship
The Presbyterian service book, published in 1993, that suggests orders and texts for various services of worship.

Book of Confessions
A volume of historic confessions of the Christian church, covering twenty centuries. Part of the Constitution, along with the *Book of Order.*

Book of Order
Contains (1) Form of Government, (2) Directory for Worship, (3) Rules of Discipline.

Call/Invitation
A "call" is extended to a prospective pastor or associate pastor by a congregation. "Invitations" are extended by session to prospective assistant pastors.

Calvinist

One who identifies with the theological views of John Calvin as set forth in *Institutes of the Christian Religion* (1536), with special stress upon God as sovereign.

Candidates

Students preparing for the ministry who have been approved by presbytery as candidates under the care of presbytery.

Catechism

The 210th General Assembly (1998) approved a new catechism for study and use in the PC(USA). There are three versions: Belonging to God: A First Catechism; The Study Catechism: Confirmation Version; and The Study Catechism: Full Version.

Celtic Cross

Traditional cross with circle superimposed where crosspieces join. Used as the logo of the former United Presbyterian Church U.S. Sometimes referred to in Scotland as the Wayside Cross.

Churches Uniting in Christ (CUIC)

A relationship among several Protestant denominations that grew out of the Consultation on Church Union (COCU). The denominations, while retaining their own identity and decision-making structures, have pledged to draw closer together in sacred things, including regular sharing of the Lord's Supper and common mission.

Deacon

Ordained office. A deacon is elected by the congregation to minister to those in need, the sick, the friendless, and any who may be in distress. The board of deacons carries out its work under the session's oversight.

Delegate/Commissioner

Delegate: any person delegated to a specific task. Commissioner: minister or elder elected to a governing body.

Directory for Worship
　　Section of the *Book of Order* that provides the standards and norms for the ordering of worship.

Dockets
　　Lists of items to be considered at a meeting.

Elder
　　Member elected by the congregation, ordained, and installed as a member of the session. May or may not currently serve actively on the session.

Full Communion Partnership
　　The relationship between the PC(USA), the Evangelical Lutheran Church in America (ELCA), the Reformed Church of America (RCA), and the United Church of Christ (UCC), whereby each denomination recognizes the others' baptisms and ministries, encourages the sharing of the Lord's Supper among their members, makes provision for the orderly exchange of ordained ministers, and commits themselves to an ongoing process of consultation and dialogue.

General Assembly
　　The highest of the four governing bodies in the Presbyterian Church (U.S.A.). The General Assemby (GA) consists of commissioners and advisory delegates, and meets once a year in the summer for a week of meetings and worship.

Governing bodies
　　Session, presbytery, synod, and General Assembly.

Moderator
　　Presiding officer of a committee, youth group, board of deacons, session, presbytery, synod, or General Assembly.

Ordination
　　The setting apart for the ministry of the Word and Sacrament or the office of elder or deacon. Persons are ordained only once.

Permanent Judicial Commission

A commission charged with hearing remedial and disciplinary cases at the presbytery, synod, and General Assembly levels.

Presbytery

The governing body above the session, defined by geographical boundaries. There are 173 presbyteries.

Robert's Rules of Order

The approved parliamentary procedure for all governing bodies.

Rules of Discipline

Section of the *Book of Order* relating to church discipline and conflict resolution.

Sacraments

Presbyterians observe two sacraments: baptism and the Lord's Supper.

Seminaries

Institutions for training prospective pastors and other church workers.

Stated Clerk

Secretary-parliamentarian at the levels of presbytery, synod, and General Assembly.

Synod

The middle governing body made up of presbytery representatives. There are 16 synods.

Trustees

Legally elected managers of a corporation. The office ordinarily relates to matters of property. Many Presbyterian churches now have unicameral systems of government, which means sessions serve concurrently as boards of trustees.

Notes

1. From *Letters to Young Churches,* translated by J. B. Phillips. The Macmillan Company. © The Macmillan Company 1947, 1957.

2. From an unofficial revision of the Confession of 1967, prepared for a Symposium on the Confession of 1967 held at Princeton, N.J., in 1982. Published in *Journal of Presbyterian History,* Spring 1983.

3. An unpublished poem by E. Louise Hermanson. Used by permission of the author.

4. Quoted in *Prayer that Prevails,* by G. Ray Jordan. © The Macmillan Company, 1958.

5. From "The Boston Affirmations," a statement prepared by members of the Boston Industrial Mission Task Force, as reprinted in *Christianity and Crisis,* February 16, 1976.

6. An unpublished poem by William S. Findley. Used by permission.

7. Margaret E. Kuhn, "Today's Deacon," in *Vanguard,* March 1972.

8. Adapted from stanza 3 of the hymn "The Sun Is on the Land and Sea," by Louis F. Benson, 1897.

9. From "Passed Thru the Waters," in *Alive and Singing.* Copyright © 1971 by Richard K. Avery and Donald C. Marsh. Used by permission.

10. From "The Job," by Badger Clark. Used by permission.

11. From "Psalm Against the Darkness," by Aloysius Michael Sullivan. Copyright © 1944 by the Catholic Poetry Society.

12. From "A Declaration of Faith." Copyright 1977 by the Stated Clerk of the General Assembly, Presbyterian Church in the U.S.